ST. LOUIS
Walk of Fame

75

Great St. Louisans

ST. LOUIS WALK OF FAME: 75 Great St. Louisans

ISBN: 0-9661620-0-5

ORDERING INFORMATION:

Individual Orders
Send $18.50 plus $4.00 shipping to:

Book Order Department
St. Louis Walk of Fame
6504 Delmar
St. Louis, MO 63130

Schools and Businesses:
Write for information about quantity discounts
with bulk purchases for educational, business,
or sales promotional purposes.

*All proceeds received from the sale of this book go
directly to the non-profit St. Louis Walk of Fame.*

Visit the St. Louis Walk of Fame web site at:
www.stlouiswalkoffame.org

PRINTED IN THE UNITED STATES OF AMERICA

CONTENTS

FOREWORD

THE ST. LOUIS WALK OF FAME is a nonprofit organization founded in 1988 to provide a showcase for the cultural heritage of St. Louis and to advance the knowledge, awareness and appreciation of great St. Louisans and their accomplishments.

The Walk of Fame itself consists of sets of brass stars and bronze plaques honoring individuals from the St. Louis area who made major national contributions to our cultural heritage.

Each star features the name of an honoree; an accompanying plaque contains a brief biographical summary. The informational plaques set the St. Louis Walk of Fame apart from any project of its kind in the country, and help make it educational and inspirational as well as enjoyable. The knowledge gained from the plaques instills pride in our community.

The stars and plaques are permanently set into the sidewalks of the University City Loop, centrally located in the St. Louis area. The Walk of Fame is free of charge, open all year and easily accessible for all to enjoy.

— Joe Edwards
Founder

INTRODUCTION

BY WILLIAM F. WOO

EMBEDDED IN THE SIDEWALK along Delmar Boulevard in the Loop area of University City, Missouri, is a succession of large brass stars. Every star is accompanied in the pavement by a bronze plaque and each set commemorates the life and achievements of an extraordinary man or woman who is associated with St. Louis. Ulysses S. Grant is there, as is T.S. Eliot, Josephine Baker, Scott Joplin, Susan Blow, Stan Musial, Joseph Pulitzer, Chuck Berry, Tennessee Williams, Charles A. Lindbergh, Betty Grable and many others, 50 [now 75] in all.

Joe Edwards, proprietor of the Rock 'n Roll restaurant and pub called Blueberry Hill, conceived the St. Louis Walk of Fame as a way not only of commemorating St. Louis' many contributions to art and literature, music and science, athletics and entertainment, journalism and politics, but also as a way of adding some further enrichment to one of the country's most unusual stretches of urban thoroughfare. Thus since 1989 the Walk of Fame has paid simultaneous tribute to men and women of distinction, to a great metropolitan community and to the street where small business people earn their livings in their own ways.

For Delmar Boulevard is not so much America as it *is*, but America as it *will be*. Walk up and down it to inspect the stars and plaques, to read the names and the brief commentaries and to let memory and imagination do their work, and you see black people and brown, yellow people and white people, old people, children, men and women of ordinary aspect and youth dressed in the costumes and styles of eras that may never be—all these colors and ages and appearances, together.

Here along Delmar are all the things human beings have to have: old books, new books, hardware, good beer, arts and crafts, fresh oysters and fresh ground coffee and fresh bread, fruits and vegetables that you can pick up and shake and tap, newspapers, fresh flowers, movies, music recorded and music played live, hummus and sushi and barbecue, the delicate and colorful works of ethnic cultures and baseball cards.

America as we knew it and America as it remakes itself in the image of the world—all right here, all right now, static and in motion, up and down and all around the procession of stars, each one celebrating a St. Louisan who did something few people or none have ever done better. Miles Davis. Cool Papa Bell. William Burroughs. Masters and Johnson. Charles M. Russell and Eugene Field and more to come. The accomplishments of these men and woman in the pavement go beyond their city or their fields of endeavor; for they also have given form and meaning to the larger America that you see along Delmar Boulevard as you walk among the stars.

[William F. Woo was editor of the *St. Louis Post-Dispatch*. Part of this introduction is adapted from his keynote speech at the Walk of Fame induction ceremony in 1991.]

NOMINATION CRITERIA

NOMINEES FOR THE ST. LOUIS WALK OF FAME must fulfill two main criteria:

(1) They must have been born in St. Louis or spent their formative or creative years here.

(2) Their accomplishments must have had a national impact on our cultural heritage.

Many wonderful St. Louisans qualify for one but not the other condition. Perhaps he or she did not reside in the St. Louis area long enough to be firmly associated with the city, or did not spent formative or creative years here. Perhaps due to the nature of the person's work, his or her contributions and achievements did not have a national impact, even though the impact locally was immense.

NOMINATION PROCESS

THERE ARE APPROXIMATELY 250 GREAT ST. LOUISANS from the past and present on the list of nominees. They represent national luminaries from fields such as art, music, architecture, literature, journalism, civil rights, education, science, sports, acting, entertainment and broadcasting.

Anyone may participate in the nomination process. Simply send a letter to the St. Louis Walk of Fame office with the name, date and place of birth, and a short history of the person you wish to nominate. Include the person's St. Louis connection and a description of his or her national impact. Address your envelope as follows:

Nominations Committee
St. Louis Walk of Fame
6504 Delmar
St. Louis, MO 63130

SELECTION PROCESS

ONE HUNDRED AND TWENTY ST. LOUISANS are on the Walk of Fame selection committee. The committee includes the chancellors of all area universities, key people from local libraries, arts organizations and historical societies, media journalists, and other citizens with an informed understanding of St. Louis' cultural heritage. The selection committee is 51 percent female and 49 percent male; it is 71 percent white, 27 percent African-American, and 2 percent Asian-American. Ballots are mailed to selection committee members in the fall of each year, and the new inductees are announced the following spring.

INDUCTION CEREMONY

EACH YEAR ON THE THIRD SUNDAY IN MAY, the induction ceremony of the St. Louis Walk of Fame takes place on an outdoor stage at 6500 Delmar next to Blueberry Hill. (In the event of rain, the ceremony will be held indoors at the Tivoli Theatre, located at 6350 Delmar.) The festivities begin at 1:30 P.M. with a free concert of ragtime and Dixieland jazz, followed by the keynote address and the induction of the honorees. Always entertaining, the induction ceremony is free and everyone is invited!

INDUCTION CEREMONY, 1992

CLARK TERRY

FROM LEFT TO RIGHT: LEONARD SLATKIN, HOWARD NEMEROV, WILLIAM DANFORTH, WILLIE MAE FORD SMITH

JOHN GOODMAN

CLARENCE HARMON, 1996

KEYNOTE SPEAKERS

STAN MUSIAL, 1993

GWEN STEPHENSON, 1992

WILLIAM WOO, 1991

BLANCHE TOUHILL, 1995

HARRIETT WOODS, 1989

BILL McCLELLAN, 1997

WILLIAM DANFORTH, 1990

GREG FREEMAN, 1994

11

LOCATION

THE ST. LOUIS WALK OF FAME is set in the sidewalks along the 6200-6600 blocks of Delmar Boulevard in the University City Loop. Centrally located in the St. Louis metropolitan area, the Walk of Fame is less than 20 minutes from downtown St. Louis and from Lambert International Airport, five minutes from Clayton and within walking distance of Washington University.

There is easy access to highways 40 (I-64), I-170, I-44, Forest Park Parkway and the Delmar MetroLink Station. Parking information and a detailed map of the University City Loop are on the following page.

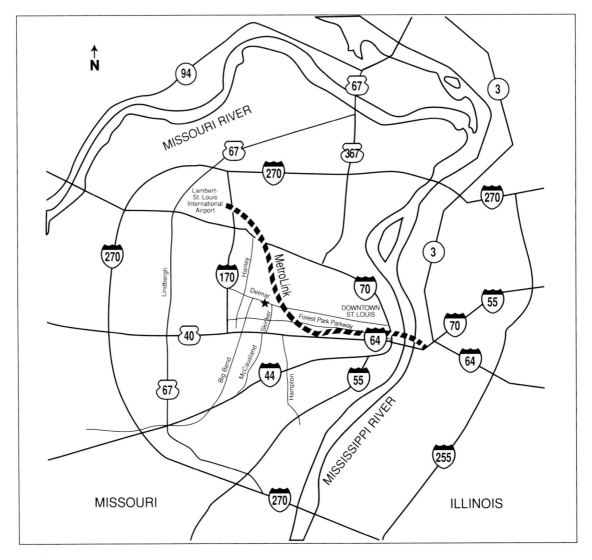

LOCATION IN DETAIL

THE UNIVERSITY CITY LOOP is a vibrant four block area that has been noted in the *St. Louis Post-Dispatch* and *The Riverfront Times* as a model of urban development. Its beautiful, tree-lined streets are home to over 90 specialty shops, diverse restaurants and pubs, book and music stores, craft and performing arts organizations, galleries and more. A multi-cultural neighborhood with a deep sense of community, a major portion of the area is designated as an Historic District.

As pictured in the map below, the Loop offers plenty of parking. There are four large, well-lighted parking lots, a parking garage with an attendant, and abundant on-street parking. Tour bus parking is available in the lot between Kingsland and Leland. MetroLink riders can get off at the Delmar station and take a four block bus or shuttle ride into the Loop.

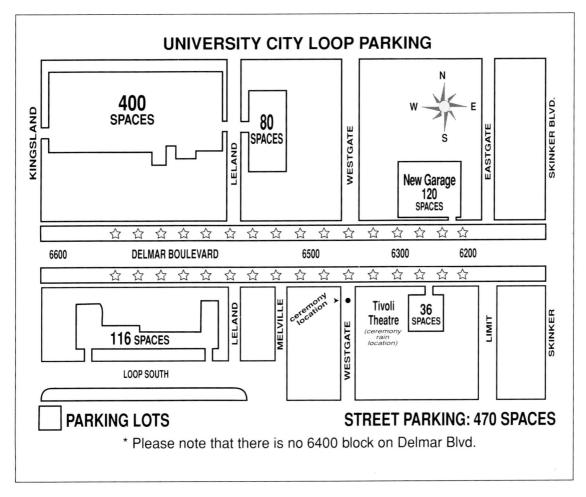

LIST OF INDUCTEES BY
FIELDS OF ACHIEVEMENT

Acting/Entertainment
Josephine Baker
Phyllis Diller
Katherine Dunham
Buddy Ebsen
Redd Foxx
John Goodman
Betty Grable
Dick Gregory
Virginia Mayo
Agnes Moorehead
Vincent Price
Shelley Winters

Art/Architecture
James Eads
Charles Eames
Al Hirschfeld
Theodore Link
Gyo Obata
Charles Russell
Ernest Trova

Broadcasting
Jack Buck
Harry Caray
Bob Costas
Joe Garagiola
Dave Garroway

General Category
Auguste Chouteau
City Founder
William Clark
Explorer
Tom Eagleton
Politics
Ulysses S. Grant
Military / U.S. President
Pierre Laclede
City Founder
Charles Lindbergh
Aviation
Dred & Harriet Scott
Civil Rights

Journalism
Elijah Lovejoy
Bill Mauldin
Joseph Pulitzer

Literature
Maya Angelou
William Burroughs
Kate Chopin
T.S. Eliot
Stanley Elkin
Eugene Field
A.E. Hotchner
William Inge
Marianne Moore
Howard Nemerov
Sara Teasdale
Mona Van Duyn
Tennessee Williams

Music
Chuck Berry
Grace Bumbry
Miles Davis
Scott Joplin
Albert King
Leonard Slatkin
Willie Mae Ford Smith
Clark Terry
Henry Townsend
Helen Traubel
Tina Turner

Science/Education
Susan Blow
Barry Commoner
Arthur Holly Compton
Carl & Gerty Cori
Masters & Johnson
Marlin Perkins
Peter Raven
Henry Shaw

Sports
Henry Armstrong
James "Cool Papa" Bell
Yogi Berra
Lou Brock
Dwight Davis
Dizzy Dean
Bob Gibson
Stan Musial
Branch Rickey

LOCATION OF STARS BY NAME

Inductee Name	Address	Inductee Name	Address
Maya Angelou	6337	Dick Gregory	6611
Henry Armstrong	6622	Al Hirschfeld	6301
Josephine Baker	6501	A.E. Hotchner	6608
James "Cool Papa" Bell	6265	William Inge	6624
Yogi Berra	6322	Scott Joplin	6510
Chuck Berry	6504	Albert King	6370
Susan Blow	6374	Pierra Laclede	6317
Lou Brock	6602	Charles Lindbergh	6519
Jack Buck	6307	Theodore Link	6617
Grace Bumbry	6319	Elijah Lovejoy	6332
William Burroughs	6362	Masters & Johnson	6380
Harry Caray	6321	Bill Mauldin	6271
Kate Chopin	6310	Virginia Mayo	6620
Auguste Chouteau	6358	Marianne Moore	6625
William Clark	6619	Agnes Moorhead	6604
Barry Commoner	6342	Stan Musial	6502
Arthur Holly Compton	6329	Howard Nemerov	6500
Carl & Gerty Cori	6605	Gyo Obata	6325
Bob Costas	6502	Marlin Perkins	6505
Dwight Davis	6621	Vincent Price	6509
Miles Davis	6314	Joseph Pulitzer	6515
Dizzy Dean	6643	Peter Raven	6605
Phyllis Diller	6366	Branch Rickey	6631
Katherine Dunham	6513	Charles Russell	6388
James Eads	6635	Dred & Harriet Scott	6647
Tom Eagleton	6633	Henry Shaw	6346
Charles Eames	6606	Leonard Slatkin	6318
Buddy Ebsen	6303	Willie Mae Ford Smith	6392
T.S. Eliot	6525	Sara Teasdale	6603
Stanley Elkin	6275	Clark Terry	6623
Eugene Field	6315	Henry Townsend	6610
Redd Foxx	6331	Helen Traubel	6601
Joe Garagiola	6328	Ernest Trova	6335
Dave Garroway	6627	Tina Turner	6378
Bob Gibson	6352	Mona Van Duyn	6273
John Goodman	6508	Tennessee Williams	6500
Betty Grable	6350	Shelly Winters	6323
Ulysses S. Grant	6394		

LOCATION OF STARS BY STREET NUMBER

NORTH SIDE OF DELMAR BLVD.			SOUTH SIDE OF DELMAR BLVD.	
Inductee Name	**Address**		**Address**	**Inductee Name**
James "Cool Papa" Bell	6265		6310	Kate Chopin
Bill Mauldin	6271		6314	Miles Davis
Mona Van Duyn	6273		6318	Leonard Slatkin
Stanley Elkin	6275		6322	Yogi Berra
Al Hirschfeld	6301		6328	Joe Garagiola
Buddy Ebsen	6303		6332	Elijah Lovejoy
Jack Buck	6307		6342	Barry Commoner
Eugene Field	6315		6346	Henry Shaw
Pierre Laclede	6317		6350	Betty Grable
Grace Bumbry	6319		6352	Bob Gibson
Harry Caray	6321		6358	Auguste Chouteau
Shelley Winters	6323		6362	William Burroughs
Gyo Obata	6325		6366	Phyllis Diller
Arthur Holly Compton	6329		6370	Albert King
Redd Foxx	6331		6374	Susan Blow
Ernest Trova	6335		6378	Tina Turner
Maya Angelou	6337		6380	Masters & Johnson
Josephine Baker	6501		6388	Charles Russell
Marlin Perkins	6505		6392	Willie Mae Ford Smith
Vincent Price	6509		6394	Ulysses S. Grant
Katherine Dunham	6513		6500	Tennessee Williams
Joseph Pulitzer	6515		6500	Howard Nemerov
Charles Lindbergh	6519		6502	Stan Musial
T.S. Eliot	6525		6502	Bob Costas
Helen Traubel	6601		6504	Chuck Berry
Sara Teasdale	6603		6508	John Goodman
Carl & Gerty Cori	6605		6510	Scott Joplin
Peter Raven	6605		6602	Lou Brock
Dick Gregory	6611		6604	Agnes Moorehead
Theodore Link	6617		6606	Charles Eames
William Clark	6619		6608	A.E. Hotchner
Dwight Davis	6621		6610	Henry Townsend
Clark Terry	6623		6620	Virginia Mayo
Marianne Moore	6625		6622	Henry Armstrong
Dave Garroway	6627		6624	William Inge
Branch Rickey	6631			
Tom Eagleton	6633			
James Eads	6635			
Dizzy Dean	6643			
Dred & Harriet Scott	6647			

DELMAR

16

LIST OF INDUCTEES BY YEAR OF BIRTH

Year	Date	Inductee Name	Year	Date	Inductee Name
1729	11-22	Pierre Laclede	1912	12-12	Henry Armstrong
1749	9-7	Auguste Chouteau	1913	5-3	William Inge
1770	8-1	William Clark	1913	7-13	Dave Garroway
1799 (circa)	Unknown	Dred Scott	1914	2-5	William Burroughs
Unknown	Unknown	Harriet Scott	1915	12-27	William Masters
1800	7-24	Henry Shaw	1916	12-18	Betty Grable
1802	11-9	Elijah Lovejoy	1917	5-28	Barry Commoner
1820	5-23	James Eads	1917	7-17	Phillis Diller
1822	4-27	Ulysses S. Grant	1920	3-1	Harry Caray
1843	6-7	Susan Blow	1920	3-1	Howard Nemerov
1847	4-10	Joseph Pulitzer	1920	6-28	A.E. Hotchner
1850	3-17	Theodore Link	1920	8-18	Shelley Winters
1850	9-2	Eugene Field	1920	11-21	Stan Musial
1851	2-8	Kate Chopin	1920	11-30	Virginia Mayo
1864	3-19	Charles Russell	1920	12-14	Clark Terry
1868	11-24	Scott Joplin	1921	5-9	Mona Van Duyn
1879	7-5	Dwight Davis	1921	10-29	Bill Mauldin
1881	12-20	Branch Rickey	1922	12-9	Redd Foxx
1884	8-8	Sara Teasdale	1923	2-28	Gyo Obata
1887	11-15	Marianne Moore	1923	4-25	Albert King
1888	9-26	T.S. Eliot	1924	8-21	Jack Buck
1892	9-10	Arthur Holly Compton	1925	2-11	Virginia Johnson
1896	8-15	Gerty Cori	1925	5-12	Yogi Berra
1896	12-5	Carl Cori	1926	2-12	Joe Garagiola
1899	6-16	Helen Traubel	1926	5-26	Miles Davis
1900	12-6	Agnes Moorehead	1926	10-18	Chuck Berry
1902	2-4	Charles Lindbergh	1927	2-19	Ernest Trova
1902	3-28	Marlin Perkins	1928	4-4	Maya Angelou
1903	5-17	Cool Papa Bell	1929	9-4	Tom Eagleton
1903	6-21	Al Hirschfeld	1930	5-11	Stanley Elkin
1904	6-23	Willie Mae Ford Smith	1932	10-12	Dick Gregory
1906	6-3	Josephine Baker	1935	11-9	Bob Gibson
1907	6-17	Charles Eames	1936	6-13	Peter Raven
1908	4-2	Buddy Ebsen	1937	1-4	Grace Bumbry
1909	6-22	Katherine Dunham	1939	6-18	Lou Brock
1909	10-27	Henry Townsend	1939	11-26	Tina Turner
1910	1-16	Dizzy Dean	1944	9-1	Leonard Slatkin
1911	3-26	Tennessee Williams	1952	3-22	Bob Costas
1911	5-27	Vincent Price	1952	6-20	John Goodman

LIST OF INDUCTEES BY MONTH AND DAY OF BIRTH

Date	Inductee Name	Date	Inductee Name
Jan. 4, 1937	Grace Bumbry	June 23, 1904	Willie Mae Ford Smith
Jan. 16, 1910	Dizzy Dean	June 28, 1920	A.E. Hotchner
Feb. 4, 1902	Charles Lindbergh	July 5, 1879	Dwight Davis
Feb. 5, 1914	William Burroughs	July 13, 1913	Dave Garroway
Feb. 8, 1851	Kate Chopin	July 17, 1917	Phyllis Diller
Feb. 11, 1925	Virginia Johnson	July 24, 1800	Henry Shaw
Feb. 12, 1926	Joe Garagiola	Aug. 1, 1770	William Clark
Feb. 19, 1927	Ernest Trova	Aug. 8, 1884	Sara Teasdale
Feb. 28, 1923	Gyo Obata	Aug. 15, 1896	Gerty Cori
Mar. 1, 1920	Harry Caray	Aug. 18, 1920	Shelley Winters
Mar. 1, 1920	Howard Nemerov	Aug. 21, 1924	Jack Buck
Mar. 17, 1850	Theodore Link	Sept. 1, 1944	Leonard Slatkin
Mar. 19, 1864	Charles Russell	Sept. 2, 1850	Eugene Field
Mar. 22, 1952	Bob Costas	Sept. 4, 1929	Tom Eagleton
Mar. 26, 1911	Tennessee Williams	Sept. 7, 1749	Auguste Chouteau
Mar. 28, 1902	Marlin Perkins	Sept. 10, 1892	Arthur Holly Compton
Apr. 2, 1908	Buddy Ebsen	Sept. 26, 1888	T.S. Eliot
Apr. 4, 1928	Maya Angelou	Oct. 12, 1932	Dick Gregory
Apr. 10, 1847	Joseph Pulitzer	Oct. 18, 1926	Chuck Berry
Apr. 25, 1923	Albert King	Oct. 27, 1909	Henry Townsend
Apr. 27, 1822	Ulysses S. Grant	Oct. 29, 1921	Bill Mauldin
May 3, 1913	William Inge	Nov. 9, 1802	Elijah Lovejoy
May 9, 1921	Mona Van Duyn	Nov. 9, 1935	Bob Gibson
May 11, 1930	Stanley Elkin	Nov. 15, 1887	Marianne Moore
May 12, 1925	Yogi Berra	Nov. 21, 1920	Stan Musial
May 17, 1903	Cool Papa Bell	Nov. 22, 1729	Pierre Laclede
May 23, 1820	James Eads	Nov. 24, 1868	Scott Joplin
May 26, 1926	Miles Davis	Nov. 26, 1939	Tina Turner
May 27, 1911	Vincent Price	Nov. 30, 1920	Virginia Mayo
May 28, 1917	Barry Commoner	Dec. 5, 1896	Carl Cori
June 3, 1906	Josephine Baker	Dec. 6, 1900	Agnes Moorehead
June 7, 1843	Susan Blow	Dec. 9, 1922	Redd Foxx
June 13, 1936	Peter Raven	Dec. 12, 1912	Henry Armstrong
June 16, 1899	Helen Traubel	Dec. 14, 1920	Clark Terry
June 17, 1907	Charles Eames	Dec. 18, 1916	Betty Grable
June 18, 1939	Lou Brock	Dec. 20, 1881	Branch Rickey
June 20, 1952	John Goodman	Dec. 27, 1915	William Masters
June 21, 1903	Al Hirschfeld	Unknown	Dred Scott
June 22, 1909	Katherine Dunham	Unknown	Harriet Scott

Dates of Induction

Inductee	Year	Acceptor
Maya Angelou	5-17-92	Eugene B. Redmond, Poet Laureate of East St. Louis
Henry Armstrong	5-21-95	Edna Nashville (Daughter)
Josephine Baker	5-20-90	Richard Martin (Nephew)
James "Cool Papa" Bell	5-19-91	Connie Brooks (Daughter)
Yogi Berra	5-17-92	Self
Chuck Berry	6-25-89	Self
Susan Blow	5-19-91	Carolyn George, President, Susan E. Blow Foundation
Lou Brock	5-15-94	Self
Jack Buck	5-19-91	Carole Buck (Wife)
Grace Bumbry	5-17-92	Benjamin Bumbry, Jr. (Brother)
William Burroughs	5-20-90	Kenn Thomas, Thomas Jefferson Library, UMSL
Harry Caray	5-16-93	Dutchie Caray (Wife)
Kate Chopin	5-20-90	George Chopin (Grandson)
Auguste Chouteau	5-16-93	Peter Michel, Missouri Historical Society
William Clark	5-19-96	Carolyn Gilman, Missouri Historical Society
Barry Commoner	5-16-93	Self
Arthur Holly Compton	5-17-92	Clifford Will, Professor & Chairman of Physics, Washington University
Carl & Gerty Cori	5-15-94	Dr. Gary Ackers, Washington University School of Medicine, Biochemistry & Molecular Biophysics
Bob Costas	5-21-95	Pam Reichman, Business Manager & Personal Assistant
Dwight Davis	5-19-96	Tom O'Neal, Founder, St. Louis Tennis Hall of Fame
Miles Davis	5-20-90	Charlie Rose, Jazz Musician
Dizzy Dean	5-18-97	Bob Forsch, Baseball Cardinal Pitching Great
Phyllis Diller	5-16-93	Self
Katherine Dunham	6-25-89	Bonita Cornute, KTVI-TV
James Eads	6-25-89	Howard Miller, History Department, UMSL
Tom Eagleton	5-18-97	Self
Charles Eames	5-15-94	Carl Safe, Washington University School of Architecture
Buddy Ebsen	5-19-91	Steve Cox, Author, *Beverly Hillbillies*
T.S. Eliot	6-25-89	Leslie Konnyu, Founder, T.S. Eliot Society
Stanley Elkin	5-19-91	Self

DATES OF INDUCTION

(CONTINUED)

Inductee	Year	Acceptor
Eugene Field	5-19-91	John Scholz, Director, Eugene Field House and Toy Museum
Redd Foxx	5-17-92	Lavell Crawford, Comedian
Joe Garagiola	5-17-92	Self
Dave Garroway	5-19-96	Paris Garroway Neurock (Daughter)
Bob Gibson	5-16-93	Stan Musial, Baseball Cardinal Hall of Famer
John Goodman	5-18-97	Self
Betty Grable	5-20-90	Audrey Birk, Childhood Friend
Ulysses S. Grant	5-20-90	Jerry Schober, National Park Service for White Haven (Grant's Home)
Dick Gregory	5-21-95	Self
Al Hirschfeld	5-16-93	Joe Edwards, St. Louis Walk of Fame
A.E. Hotchner	5-15-94	Self
William Inge	5-21-95	Henry Schvey, Chairman, Performing Arts Department, Washington University
Scott Joplin	6-25-89	Annette Bridges, Site Administrator, Scott Joplin House
Albert King	5-16-93	Chuck Berry, Rock & Roll Hall of Famer
Pierre Laclede	5-16-93	Katherine Corbett, Missouri Historical Society
Charles Lindbergh	6-25-89	Judy Little, President, University City Historical Society
Theodore Link	5-21-95	Carolyn Toft, Executive Director, Landmarks Association
Elijah Lovejoy	5-17-92	Reverend Robert Tabscott, President, Elijah Lovejoy Society
Masters & Johnson	5-19-91	Selves
Bill Mauldin	5-19-91	Martin Quigley (Author)
Virginia Mayo	5-19-96	Self
Marianne Moore	5-19-96	Professor Dan Shea, Chairman, English Department, Washington University
Agnes Moorehead	5-15-94	Carrie Houk, St. Louis Film Partnership
Stan Musial	6-25-89	Joe Edwards, St. Louis Walk of Fame
Howard Nemerov	5-20-90	Self

DATES OF INDUCTION

(CONTINUED)

Inductee	Year	Acceptor
Gyo Obata	5-17-92	Self
Marlin Perkins	5-20-90	Carol Perkins (Wife)
Vincent Price	6-25-89	Barbara Gay (Niece)
Joseph Pulitzer	6-25-89	William F. Woo, Editor, St. Louis Post-Dispatch
Peter Raven	5-21-95	Self
Branch Rickey	5-18-97	Stephen S. Adams III (Grandson)
Charles Russell	5-19-91	Will Fulkerson (Relative)
Dred & Harriet Scott	5-18-97	Kathryn Nelson, Educator and Activist; Stephanie Gathright (Great-great Granddaughter)
Henry Shaw	5-16-93	Dr. Peter Raven, Director, Missouri Botanical Garden
Leonard Slatkin	5-20-90	Self
Willie Mae Ford Smith	5-20-90	Self
Sara Teasdale	5-15-94	Dr. David Hadas, English Department, Washington University
Clark Terry	5-19-96	Self
Henry Townsend	5-21-95	Self
Helen Traubel	5-15-94	Charles Mackay, Managing Director, Opera Theater of St. Louis
Ernest Trova	5-17-92	Adam Aronson, Art Collector & Patron
Tina Turner	5-19-91	Oliver Sain, St. Louis Rhythm & Blues Music Great
Mona Van Duyn	5-16-93	Self
Tennessee Williams	6-25-89	Dakin Williams (Brother)
Shelley Winters	5-17-92	Self

MAYA ANGELOU

BORN APRIL 4, 1928

Maya Angelou, born Marguerite Johnson in St. Louis, was raised in segregated rural Arkansas. Her best-selling account of that upbringing, *I Know Why the Caged Bird Sings*, won critical acclaim in 1970. A leading literary voice of the African-American community, Angelou wrote a dozen more books of prose and poetry, earning Pulitzer Prize and National Book Award nominations. She was also nominated for an Emmy Award for her acting in *Roots*, and her screenplay *Georgia. Georgia* was the first by a black woman to be filmed. An eminent lecturer, Maya Angelou became a professor of American Studies at Wake Forest University in 1981.

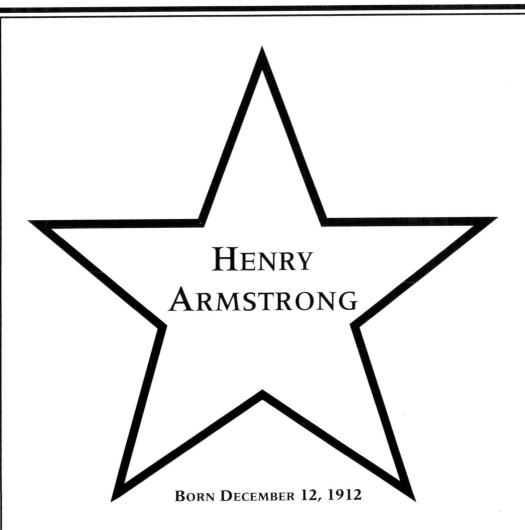

HENRY ARMSTRONG

BORN DECEMBER 12, 1912

The only boxer to hold world titles in three weight classes simultaneously, Henry Armstrong moved to St. Louis as a young boy and was an honor student at Vashon High School. Known as "Perpetual Motion," he dominated feather, welter and lightweight opponents with his "blackout" punch, relentless attack and incredible stamina. After 152 victories in 14 years, Armstrong retired in 1945. Returning to St. Louis, he became a minister, helped run the Herbert Hoover Boys' Club and trained young boxers. One of the first inductees when the Boxing Hall of Fame opened in 1954, Henry Armstrong is considered one of the top three boxers of all time.

JOSEPHINE BAKER

BORN JUNE 3, 1906

As a child in St. Louis, Josephine Baker rummaged for coal behind Union Station and for food behind Soulard Market. At age 13 she waitressed at the Chauffeurs' Club on Pine Street and danced with a minstrel band. In 1925 she went to Paris with the Revue Nègre. She starred in the Folies-Bergère the next season and became one of France's best-loved entertainers. During World War II, she was a heroine of the Resistance, earning the Légion d'Honneur. A French citizen, she was an activist for civil rights in the United States. On her death in 1975, she was given an unprecedented state funeral in Paris.

COOL PAPA BELL

BORN MAY 17, 1903

Major league baseball was closed to blacks until 1947, relegating some of the game's best players to the Negro Leagues. One of them was James Thomas Bell, who joined the St. Louis Stars in 1922. Nicknamed Cool Papa for his composure, Bell played and coached professional baseball for 29 years. Known as the fastest player ever, Cool Papa often stole two bases on one pitch or scored from second on a sacrifice fly. Satchel Paige said Bell could turn off the light and "be in bed before the room was dark." He batted .400 several times and stole 175 bases in one year. Cool Papa Bell was inducted into the Baseball Hall of Fame in 1974.

YOGI BERRA

BORN MAY 12, 1925

Lawrence Peter Berra grew up on Elizabeth Street in the St. Louis neighborhood called The Hill. After heroic service in World War II, Yogi Berra joined the Yankees late in the 1946 season and hit a home run in his first at-bat. For the next 17 years he anchored the greatest dynasty in baseball history, winning 10 of 14 World Series. Famed for fractured English in quotes such as "It ain't over 'til it's over," Berra was a three-time MVP. He holds numerous World Series records, such as 71 hits. As a manager and coach, he led his teams to five World Series, winning three. In 1973, Yogi Berra was inducted into the Baseball Hall of Fame.

CHUCK BERRY

BORN OCTOBER 18, 1926

Hailed as the "Father of Rock & Roll," Chuck Berry's signature guitar work, poetic songwriting, and inspired showmanship have influenced every Rock & Roll musician to follow him. Beginning with "Maybellene" in 1955, he recorded a series of hits that defined the standards of the genre. He was the first person inducted into the Rock & Roll Hall of Fame, and is a member of the Songwriters Hall of Fame. His song "Johnny B. Goode" is on the copper records aboard the Voyager Space Probes, launched into outer space in 1977 to reach out to the universe with the best of our culture.

SUSAN BLOW

BORN JUNE 7, 1843

The average poor child in 1860s St. Louis completed three years of school before being forced to begin work at age 10. Susan Elizabeth Blow addressed that problem by offering education to children earlier. Applying Friedrich Froebel's theories, she opened the United States' first successful public kindergarten at St. Louis' Des Peres School in 1873. Blow taught children in the morning and teachers in the afternoon. By 1883 every St. Louis public school had a kindergarten, making the city a model for the nation. Devoting her life to early education, Susan Blow was instrumental in establishing kindergartens throughout America.

LOU
BROCK

BORN JUNE 18, 1939

The greatest base stealer of his era, St. Louis Cardinal Louis Clark Brock was only the 14th player to have 3,000 hits. After three seasons with the Chicago Cubs, Brock joined the Cardinals in 1964 and fueled their World Series victory. During his 19-year career, the outfielder stole an unprecedented 938 bases and broke several World Series records, including hitting .391 in over 20 World Series games. Exemplifying the spirit of baseball on and off the field, Brock earned the Roberto Clemente and the Jackie Robinson Awards, among many others. A Cardinal until he retired, Lou Brock entered the Baseball Hall of Fame on the first ballot in 1985.

JACK BUCK

BORN AUGUST 21, 1924

John Francis Buck joined Harry Caray in 1954 to announce St. Louis Cardinals baseball games. Their fourteen-year partnership has been called the greatest broadcast team in baseball history. Buck went on to become the anchor of the Cardinals broadcast team and sports director of KMOX radio. Capping each Redbird victory with a cry of "That's a winner," Buck's wit, precision and enthusiasm earned him CBS-TV's top play-by-play spot. Also an experienced football commentator, he announced eight Super Bowls. In 1987 Jack Buck was inducted into Baseball's Hall of Fame.

GRACE
BUMBRY

BORN JANUARY 4, 1937

Grace Ann Bumbry grew up at 1703 Goode Ave. in St. Louis. She joined the Union Memorial Methodist Church's choir at eleven, and sang at Sumner High School. She was a 1954 winner on the "Arthur Godfrey Talent Scouts." After her concert debut in London in 1959, Bumbry debuted with the Paris Opera the next year. In 1961 Richard Wagner's grandson featured her in Bayreuth, Germany's Wagner Festival. The first black to sing there, Bumbry was an international sensation and won the Wagner Medal. A mezzo-soprano who also successfully sang the soprano repertoire, Grace Bumbry recorded on four labels and sang in concerts worldwide.

WILLIAM BURROUGHS

BORN FEBRUARY 5, 1914

Born at 4664 Pershing Ave., William Burroughs attended Community School and John Burroughs School. He was a cub reporter for the *St. Louis Post-Dispatch* in 1935. During World War II, Burroughs met Jack Kerouac and Allen Ginsberg, forming the core of the "Beat Generation." An author and visual artist, he is best-known for his writing, which is radically unconventional in technique and content. It often has been banned. His 1960 novel, *The Naked Lunch*, influenced an entire generation. Burroughs was inducted into the American Academy and Institute of Arts and Letters in 1983.

HARRY CARAY

BORN MARCH 1, 1920

Born Harry Christopher Carabina, he grew up at 1909 LaSalle Street in St. Louis and attended Dewey School and Webster Groves High School. He played on two local semi-pro baseball teams before starting his radio career. After announcing both Cardinals and Browns away games in 1945, the effusive Caray, renowned for yelling "Holy Cow" after big plays, broadcast for the Cardinals from 1947 to 1969. One of baseball's best-loved announcers, Caray then called Oakland A's and Chicago White Sox games before capping his career with the Chicago Cubs. In 1989 Harry Caray was inducted into the broadcasters' wing of the Baseball Hall of Fame.

KATE CHOPIN

BORN FEBRUARY 8, 1851

Katherine O'Flaherty, a member of one of St. Louis' oldest families, attended the St. Louis Academy of the Sacred Heart. When she married New Orleans native Oscar Chopin, she encountered the Creole culture which provided settings for many of her works. She wrote more than 100 short stories in the 1890s, and hosted a literary salon in her home at 3317 Morgan Street. Her 1899 novel, *The Awakening*, was condemned for its frank treatment of a young woman's sexual and artistic growth. Now it is recognized both for the quality of the writing and for its importance as an early feminist work.

AUGUSTE CHOUTEAU

BORN SEPTEMBER 7, 1749

Born René Auguste Chouteau in New Orleans, he was raised by his stepfather, Pierre Laclède, and his mother, Marie Thérèse Chouteau. As Laclede's clerk and lieutenant, the 14-year-old Chouteau led the workers who began building St. Louis on February 15, 1764. He prospered as the village grew into a commercial hub, adapting to Spanish rule in 1770 and U.S. control in 1804. Diversifying into banking and real estate as the fur trade declined, Chouteau, the town's business and social leader, was the first board of trustees chairman upon its incorporation in 1809. As an early historian of the city wrote, "Laclede founded, and Auguste Chouteau built, St. Louis."

WILLIAM CLARK

BORN AUGUST 1, 1770

After the Louisiana Purchase in 1803, Thomas Jefferson asked William Clark and Meriwether Lewis to explore the newly-acquired but uncharted northwest. An Army captain, Clark set off with Lewis from St. Charles on May 14, 1804 and vividly chronicled their 28-month trek to the Pacific and back in his drawings and journal. He then lived in St. Louis until his death, serving as governor of the Missouri Territory and as Superintendent of Indian Affairs. Mourned as a great leader, his funeral procession was a mile long. The Arch stands on the spot of Lewis and Clark's return, a monument to the westward expansion pioneered by William Clark.

BARRY COMMONER

BORN MAY 28, 1917

Barry Commoner joined the faculty of Washington University in St. Louis in 1947. In 34 years there he explored viral function and led cellular research with implications for cancer diagnosis. Alarmed in the early 1950s by the health risks posed by atomic testing, Commoner helped found the St. Louis Committee for Nuclear Information. In 1966 he established the Center for the Biology of Natural Systems to study man's relationship with the environment. The author of nine books and the 1980 Citizens' Party presidential candidate, Barry Commoner, a pioneer in the creation of the environmental movement, was termed the "Paul Revere of Ecology."

ARTHUR HOLLY COMPTON

BORN SEPTEMBER 10, 1892

Arthur Holly Compton, a science prodigy, built and flew a glider at age 18. In 1920 he became a professor and head of the physics department at Washington University. There he deduced that X-rays, known to be waves, also act like particles. He proved it with an experiment showing the scattering action now called the Compton Effect. For that fundamental discovery, Compton won the 1927 Nobel Prize. After directing the World War II research that led to the atomic bomb, he returned to Washington University in 1945 as chancellor. In 1991 NASA named its new orbiting gamma-ray observatory after Arthur Holly Compton.

CARL & GERTY CORI

BORN DECEMBER 5, 1896
AND AUGUST 15, 1896

Carl Ferdinand Cori and Gerty Theresa Radnitz earned medical degrees from the German University of Prague in 1920 and married later that year. After they joined the Washington University School of Medicine in 1931, their discovery of the mechanism for blood glucose regulation earned them the Nobel Prize in 1947. Gerty Cori was the first American woman to be so honored. In addition, six eventual Nobel laureates received training in their laboratory. Carl Cori said of their remarkable collaboration: "Our efforts have been largely complementary, and one without the other would not have gone so far..."

BOB COSTAS

BORN MARCH 22, 1952

At age 22, Bob Costas joined KMOX radio in 1974 to announce St. Louis Spirits' basketball games. During his seven years at KMOX, he honed the skills which fueled his career's meteoric rise. His intelligence, humor and presence led to a longtime union with NBC-TV, where he anchored the Olympics and showed his mastery of football, basketball and baseball, his first love. By age 40, Costas repeatedly had won the major sportscasting awards and proven his versatility with his acclaimed TV interview show, "Later." Despite a demanding travel schedule, Bob Costas and his family chose to remain in St. Louis as he became a preeminent broadcast journalist.

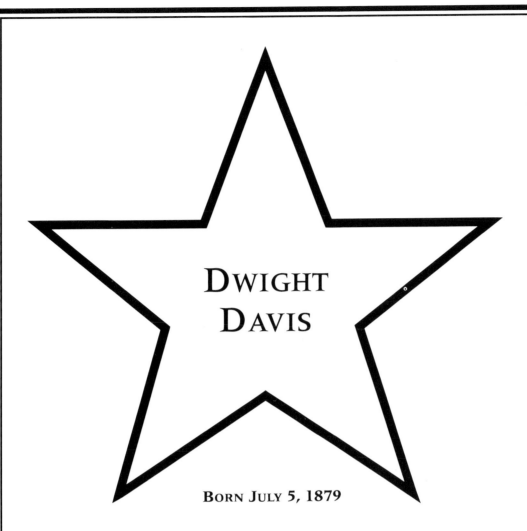

DWIGHT DAVIS

BORN JULY 5, 1879

The founder of tennis' Davis Cup, Dwight Davis was born in St. Louis. He was one of his era's best players and won several titles while at Harvard. In 1900, he founded the international competition that came to bear his name and captained the first U.S. team, which won the cup. He played in the 1904 Olympics and became St. Louis Parks Commissioner in 1911, building dozens of free tennis courts. Davis later served the game he loved as U.S. Lawn Tennis Association president, and his country as Secretary of War and Governor-General of the Philippines. The first great tennis ambassador, Dwight Davis entered the Tennis Hall of Fame in 1956.

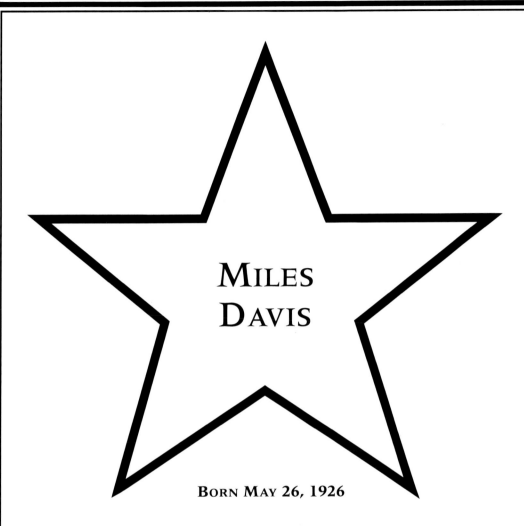

MILES DAVIS

BORN MAY 26, 1926

The year after his birth in Alton, Illinois, Miles Davis moved to East St. Louis. He played trumpet in the jazz band at Lincoln High School and was a member of Eddie Randle's Blues Devils (a.k.a. the Rhumboogie Orchestra). By 1948 he led his own bop groups in New York. One of jazz' great bandleaders and arrangers, his milestone recordings include *Birth of the Cool, Kind of Blue* and *Bitches Brew*. The *Encyclopedia of Jazz* calls him "the most consistently innovative musician in jazz from the late 1940s through the 1960s." The Miles Davis Quintet is considered one of the outstanding groups of all time.

DIZZY DEAN

BORN JANUARY 16, 1910

Known for his homespun wit and good-natured bravado, Jay Hanna "Dizzy" Dean was perhaps the most colorful member of the Cardinals' famed "Gas House Gang." With his blazing fastball he won 30 games in 1934, earning MVP honors and leading the Cardinals to a World Series victory. He won an amazing 120 games in his first five full seasons, but his career was cut short by injury. Dean moved on to announce radio broadcasts of Cardinals and Browns games, and later to television's game of the week, where his keen analysis and informal speech charmed the nation. Dizzy Dean was inducted into the Baseball Hall of Fame in 1953.

PHYLLIS DILLER

BORN JULY 17, 1917

Born Phyllis Ada Driver, she combined wild costumes, un-
tamed hair and a raucous laugh with self-deprecating mono-
logues to create one of comedy's most popular characters. A
1955 club booking skyrocketed her to success: scheduled for
two weeks, she stayed 89. After moving to Webster Groves in
1961, Diller honed her act in St. Louis clubs such as Gaslight
Square's Crystal Palace. Mid-1960s television routines featur-
ing "Fang," her imaginary husband, brought national acclaim.
In addition to her television, film and stage work, Phyllis Diller
made five records, wrote four best-selling books and per-
formed on piano with over 100 symphony orchestras.

KATHERINE DUNHAM

BORN JUNE 22, 1909

While studying anthropology at the University of Chicago, Katherine Dunham was also active as a dancer. Field trips to the West Indies allowed her to study native dances and folklore, which she incorporated into her work to form an exotic and unique repertoire. Following an acclaimed dance career in New York, she moved to East St. Louis in 1967, where she established the Performing Arts Training Center. The Katherine Dunham Museum and the Katherine Dunham Children's Workshop continue to expose new generations to the work of this great dancer and choreographer.

JAMES EADS

BORN MAY 23, 1820

The great Mississippi River bridge which bears his name is the best known of this self-educated genius' achievements. In addition, at age 22, James Eads devised the first diving bell to salvage sunken cargoes from the bottom of the river. When the Civil War began, he conceived of a fleet of armored riverboats, persuaded the Navy of its necessity, and then built the boats, which were used to capture Forts Henry and Donelson in February, 1862 — the first victories for the Union. His final engineering marvel was the system of jetties that opened the mouth of the Mississippi to seagoing ships.

TOM EAGLETON

BORN SEPTEMBER 4, 1929

Raised at 4608 Tower Grove Place, Thomas Eagleton was only 27 when elected St. Louis Circuit Attorney. He served as Missouri's Attorney General and Lieutenant Governor, won a U.S. Senate seat in 1968, and sought the Vice Presidency in 1972. He was instrumental to the Senate's passage of the Clean Air and Water Acts, and sponsored the Eagleton Amendment, which halted the bombing in Cambodia and effectively ended American involvement in the Vietnam War. After three Senate terms, Eagleton returned to St. Louis as an attorney, political commentator, and Washington University professor. The U.S. Courthouse in downtown St. Louis was named for Thomas Eagleton, a devoted Missouri citizen.

CHARLES EAMES

BORN JUNE 17, 1907

A revolutionary designer, Charles Eames was born in St. Louis and studied architecture at Washington University. He settled in Venice, California, where he designed some of the most innovative furniture of the post-War modern period with his wife Ray Kaiser. Exemplified by the Eames Chair with its molded seat and back, Eames' furniture combined simplicity and elegance, comfort and technology. Over six million of the chairs were made. Often with Ray, Eames also designed toys, buildings and fabrics, and made almost 50 educational films. Charles Eames was elected to the Academy and Institute of Arts and Letters in 1977.

BUDDY EBSEN

BORN APRIL 2, 1908

Buddy Ebsen gained worldwide fame in the 1960s as Jed Clampett, the central character on "The Beverly Hillbillies," one of the most popular comedy series in television history. He was born Christian Ludolf Ebsen Jr. in Belleville, Illinois, where his father ran a dancing school. In 1928 Ebsen danced in a Ziegfeld production on Broadway. Though he preferred working before live audiences, he moved to Hollywood in 1935 and became a movie star. A published songwriter and playwright, Buddy Ebsen is also remembered for his television roles as Georgie Russell on "Davy Crockett" in the 1950s and as "Barnaby Jones" in the 1970s.

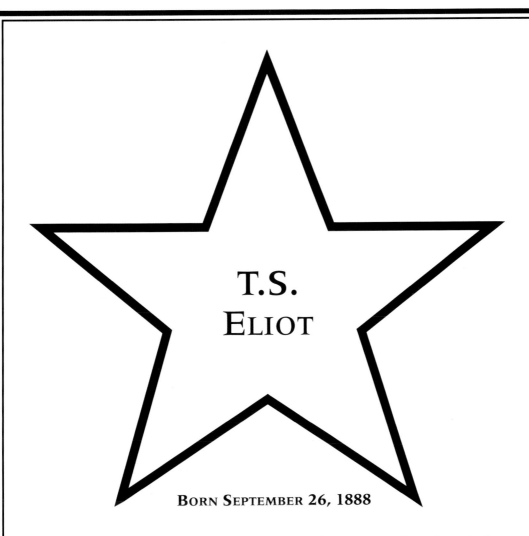

T.S. ELIOT

BORN SEPTEMBER 26, 1888

The grandson of the founder of Washington University, T. S. Eliot was born in St. Louis and attended Smith Academy here. He is best known as a poet and critic, and his *The Wasteland* is one of the most influential works of the twentieth century. Other noted compositions include "Portrait of a Lady," "The Love Song of J. Alfred Prufrock," "The Hollow Men," "Ash Wednesday," and "Four Quartets." He received the Nobel Prize for Literature in 1948, and the American Medal of Freedom in 1965.

STANLEY ELKIN

BORN MAY 11, 1930

Since his first novel was published in 1964, Stanley Lawrence Elkin's literary stature has grown unabated. A *New York Times* reviewer said, "No serious funny writer in this country can match him." Elkin became an English instructor at Washington University in St. Louis in 1960 and a professor in 1969. A member of the American Academy and Institute of Arts and Letters, he received Guggenheim and Rockefeller Foundation fellowships, the Longview Foundation Award, and the Paris Review Humor Prize. Elkin's novella, "The Bailbondsman," was made into a movie. In 1982 Stanley Elkin won the National Book Critics Circle Award.

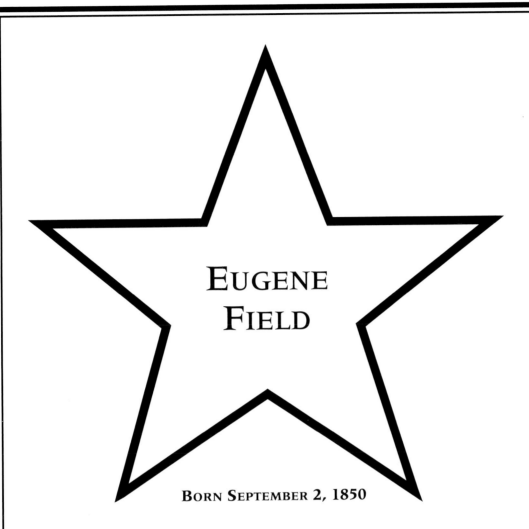

EUGENE FIELD

BORN SEPTEMBER 2, 1850

Eugene Field, born at 634 South Broadway in St. Louis, became a reporter for the *St. Louis Evening Journal* in 1873. Over the next decade he developed the charming and witty style that would make him America's foremost columnist. The *Chicago Morning News* hired him in 1883 to write "what I please on any subject I please." Although the resulting daily column, "Sharps and Flats," remains a journalistic milestone, Field is remembered mainly for his children's verses. In rhymes such as "The Duel," "Little Boy Blue," and "Wynken, Blynken, and Nod," Eugene Field captured the magic and wonder of a child's imagination.

REDD FOXX

BORN DECEMBER 9, 1922

Redd Foxx starred in "Sanford and Son," one of television's most popular comedy series in the 1970s. Born John Elroy Sanford in St. Louis, he left home at age 16 to join a New York street band. Called Red for his complexion, he adopted a baseball star's name to become Redd Foxx. Honing his comic skills in the 1940s, he became one of the nation's funniest nightclub comics, although his racy language limited his exposure. His 50 off-color "party" records reached a larger audience, selling more than 20,000,000 copies. A dramatic role in the 1970 film *Cotton Comes to Harlem* paved the way to television stardom for Redd Foxx.

JOE GARAGIOLA

BORN FEBRUARY 12, 1926

Joseph Henry Garagiola grew up on Elizabeth Street in the St. Louis neighborhood called The Hill. Signed at 16 by Branch Rickey, Garagiola played for the Cardinals in five seasons, including the 1946 championship year. After his pro career ended in 1954, he joined St. Louis radio station KMOX and broadcast Cardinals games the next year. After moving to the Yankees, Garagiola called baseball for NBC for 27 years. Two stints with the "Today Show" capped his illustrious broadcast career. A 1973 winner of television's Peabody Award, Joe Garagiola entered the broadcasters' wing of the Baseball Hall of Fame in 1991.

DAVE GARROWAY

BORN JULY 13, 1913

Moving to St. Louis at age 14, David Garroway attended University City High School and Washington University. After training as a radio announcer while an NBC page in New York, he worked in Pittsburgh and then Chicago, where he returned after serving in World War II. His popular jazz radio show led to "Garroway at Large," perhaps the most innovative early television variety show. Recognizing the appeal of his unconventional and relaxed manner, NBC chose him in 1952 as the first host of "Today," the original national morning show. Transatlantic telecasts and an on-air chimpanzee exemplified the originality of David Garroway, the man who helped wake up a nation.

BOB GIBSON

BORN NOVEMBER 9, 1935

Robert Gibson, once a Harlem Globetrotter, pitched for the St. Louis Cardinals from 1959 until he retired in 1975. Known for his fastball, he struck out 3,117 batters. In his 1968 MVP season, Bob Gibson pitched 28 complete games and 13 shutouts while setting a National League record with a 1.12 e.r.a. Pitching in three World Series, Gibson was the MVP of the Cardinals' two championships. His Series records include seven consecutive complete-game wins and 17 strikeouts in one game. Winner of nine Gold Gloves and two Cy Young Awards, he was also a feared hitter. In 1981 Bob Gibson was inducted into the Baseball Hall of Fame.

JOHN GOODMAN

BORN JUNE 20, 1952

A native son of Affton in St. Louis County, John Goodman studied drama at Southwest Missouri State and later made his mark with distinctive, often hilarious character performances in films such as *True Stories* and *Raising Arizona*. Drawing on his St. Louis roots for inspiration, Goodman starred from 1988-97 as Dan, the lovable, working-class husband on the acclaimed television series "Roseanne." Also a talented stage actor, Goodman moved to leading roles in films such as *The Babe* and *The Flintstones*. Admired by his peers and immensely popular with his fans, John Goodman's work reveals a gifted, down-to-earth actor with tremendous range.

BETTY GRABLE

BORN DECEMBER 18, 1916

Betty Grable was born at 3858 Lafayette Ave. in St. Louis and moved to the Forest Park Hotel in 1920. She entered Clark's Dancing School at age 3 and attended Mary Institute. When only 12 she went to Hollywood and got her first film role the next year. She acted in 42 films, including *Tin Pan Alley, Moon Over Miami* and *Coney Island*. Because of her world-renowned swimsuit poster, owned by one out of every five U.S. servicemen in World War II, her legs were insured for $1,000,000. Betty Grable was Hollywood's top draw in 1943, and was reported to be the highest paid woman in the United States.

ULYSSES S. GRANT

BORN APRIL 27, 1822

Upon graduating from West Point in 1843, U. S. Grant was assigned to Jefferson Barracks, near St. Louis. There he married Julia Dent, whose family estate, White Haven, was nearby. He left the army in 1854 to work his wife's farm, which he called "Hard Scrabble." He left after four years to open a real-estate agency in St. Louis. Appointed brigadier general by President Lincoln early in the Civil War, Grant captured Forts Donelson and Henry in February 1862. After further successes he was named commander of the Union army, which he led to victory. He became the 18th president of the United States in 1869.

DICK GREGORY

BORN OCTOBER 12, 1932

Born in St. Louis, Dick Gregory grew up at 1803 N. Taylor Ave. shining shoes to help feed his family. At Sumner High School, he led a march against conditions in segregated schools and set a state record in track. As a star comedian in the early 1960s, he used biting racial satire and shunned the stereotypes of early black comics. Prompted by Martin Luther King, Jr., he became a civil rights and anti-war leader, running for president in 1968 and fasting for human rights both here and abroad. Bringing wit and dedication to countless causes for decades, Dick Gregory started the "Campaign For Human Dignity" in 1992 to fight crime in St. Louis neighborhoods.

AL
HIRSCHFELD

BORN JUNE 21, 1903

Albert Hirschfeld was born in a house on Kensington Avenue in St. Louis. His family moved to New York when he was 12, and by age 18 he was artistic director at Selznick Pictures. After the *New York Times* printed one of his theater sketches in 1927, Hirschfeld emerged as a master of the line drawing. For over six decades he captured the essence of the theater's personalities with a few pen strokes. Often drawn in a dark theater, Hirschfeld's works became intrinsic to Broadway culture. Assessing their stature, one critic wrote, "There are just two forms of fame on Broadway: seeing your name in lights, and more significantly, to be drawn by Hirschfeld."

A.E. HOTCHNER

BORN JUNE 28, 1920

Born in St. Louis, Aaron Edward Hotchner grew up in the Westgate Hotel at Delmar and Kingshighway, and attended Soldan High School. A 1941 Washington University Law School graduate, he served as a military journalist before becoming a successful editor, novelist, playwright and biographer. Respected for giving all profits from a joint venture with actor Paul Newman to charities and the arts, Hotchner is best known for *Papa Hemingway*, his biography of close friend Ernest Hemingway. *King Of The Hill*, A.E. Hotchner's evocative novel about growing up in St. Louis during the Great Depression, was captured on film in 1993.

WILLIAM INGE

BORN MAY 3, 1913

Born in Independence, Kansas, William Inge taught at Stephens College before coming to St. Louis as the *Star-Times* drama critic in 1943. Encouraged and inspired by Tennessee Williams, Inge finished his first play in 1947. While teaching at Washington University from 1946-1949, he wrote the award winning *Come Back, Little Sheba*. Like *Bus Stop* (1955) and the Pulitzer Prize-winning *Picnic* (1953), it earned acclaim on Broadway and in Hollywood. His screenplay *Splendor in the Grass* won an Academy Award in 1962. The dominant playwright of the 1950s, William Inge captured the essence of Midwestern life.

SCOTT JOPLIN

BORN NOVEMBER 24, 1868

In the 1880s & 90s, as ragtime music evolved from the African rhythms of its creators' heritage, its greatest composer, Scott Joplin, was often in St. Louis, playing piano in the bawdy houses and saloons of Market and Chestnut streets. He moved to Sedalia, Missouri in 1896 to work at the Maple Leaf Club, which gave its name to one of his most popular rags. Returning to St. Louis in 1901, Joplin lived at 2658-A Morgan (later re-named Delmar Blvd.). His more than 50 published works include "The Entertainer" and "The Cascades," inspired by the waterfalls of the 1904 Worlds Fair. In 1976 a special Pulitzer Prize was awarded for his opera, *Treemonisha*.

ALBERT KING

BORN APRIL 25, 1923

Born Albert Nelson, he was a farm laborer who became a premier blues guitarist. Self-taught, first on a one-string "diddley-bow" and then on a guitar he made from a cigar box, King played left-handed and upside down. In 1956 he moved to Lovejoy, Illinois, across the river from St. Louis. King perfected his searing guitar sound in the historic 1950s and 60s St. Louis blues and R&B scene. In 1966 he signed with the Stax label, where he recorded such classics as "Crosscut Saw" and "Born Under A Bad Sign." After a legendary 1968 Fillmore West concert series and recording, Albert King was called "the most-imitated blues guitarist in the world."

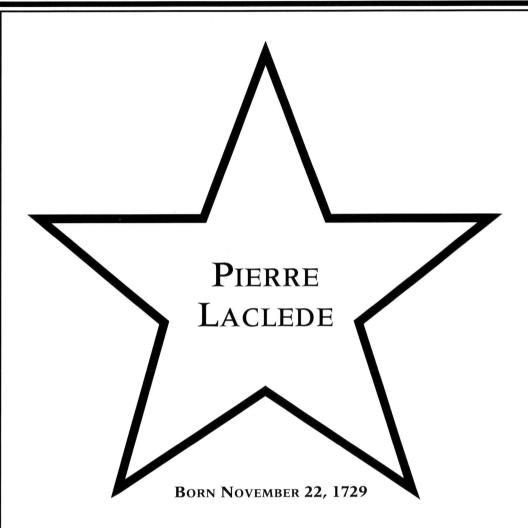

PIERRE LACLEDE

BORN NOVEMBER 22, 1729

French-born Pierre Laclède Liguest arrived in New Orleans in 1755. He ventured up the Mississippi in 1763 to build a trading post after his firm won trading rights in the upper Louisiana Territory. Choosing a site near the mouth of the Missouri, he sent his stepson, Auguste Chouteau, to start the settlement in February 1764. Naming it St. Louis, Laclede laid out streets, made property assignments and governed until territorial officials arrived in October 1765. Laclede, who brought his library to the wild, owned the town's first industry, a water-powered mill. St. Louis' first citizen, Pierre Laclede envisioned his village becoming "one of the finest cities in America."

CHARLES LINDBERGH

BORN FEBRUARY 4, 1902

One of the finest fliers of his time, Charles Lindbergh was the chief pilot for the first St. Louis to Chicago airmail route, in April 1926. While based at Lambert Field, he conceived of an airplane that could fly from New York to Paris, and persuaded a group of St. Louis businessmen to finance the project. The result was the immortal "Spirit of St. Louis," which he flew across the Atlantic on May 20-21, 1927. The feat made Lindbergh a national hero, and raised public awareness of aviation's potential to an unprecedented level.

THEODORE LINK

BORN MARCH 17, 1850

One of the city's greatest architects, German-born Theodore Link came to St. Louis in 1873. He designed over 100 buildings, including his home at 5900 West Cabanne Place, mansions at 29 and 38 Portland Place, and Grace Methodist Church on Skinker Blvd. He also designed the Mississippi State Capitol and Louisiana State University. Link's crowning achievement was St. Louis' Union Station. Completed in 1894, it was the largest station of its time and is considered an architectural "jewel." The first to use electric light decoratively and a leader of the Romanesque Revival movement, Theodore Link left St. Louis a grand and enduring legacy.

ELIJAH LOVEJOY

BORN NOVEMBER 9, 1802

Elijah Parish Lovejoy, a Presbyterian minister and editor of the *St. Louis Observer*, believed that slavery was a sin. First calling for gradual emancipation, he later became an abolitionist, but in the violent climate of 1830s St. Louis, neither stand was tolerated by slavery's proponents. Although threatened, Lovejoy insisted on the public's right to "Hear both sides and let the right triumph." Seeking safety, he moved to Alton, Illinois, but mobs there smashed three presses. Defending a fourth *Observer* press in 1837, Lovejoy was murdered, shocking the nation. In giving his life for freedom of the press, Elijah Lovejoy gave us a better knowledge of its value.

**MASTERS &
JOHNSON**

**BORN DECEMBER 27, 1915
AND FEBRUARY 11, 1925**

William Howell Masters began researching sexual function at the Washington University School of Medicine in 1954. Virginia Eshelman Johnson joined him three years later. Their investigation of the physical aspects of sexuality produced some of the first reliable data in the field. *Human Sexual Response*, Masters and Johnson's first book, was published for the medical community but became a best seller. They opened the Masters & Johnson Institute in 1964 to provide sex therapy and counseling based on their findings. The research, books and media activities of Masters and Johnson profoundly affected American society.

BILL
MAULDIN

BORN OCTOBER 29, 1921

William Henry Mauldin joined the Army newsletter *Stars and Stripes* as a cartoonist during World War II. There he perfected Joe and Willie, the muddy, weary "dogfaces" who portrayed the drabness of the foot soldier's life. Despised by the conservative brass as disrespectful but loved by G.I.s as their own, the cartoons won Bill Mauldin a 1945 Pulitzer Prize. A self-styled "stirrer-upper," Mauldin joined the *St. Louis Post-Dispatch* in 1958. Dubbed "the hottest editorial brush in the U.S.," he won his second Pulitzer Prize that year. Syndicated in over 250 newspapers, Bill Mauldin battled injustice and pretense with irony and humor.

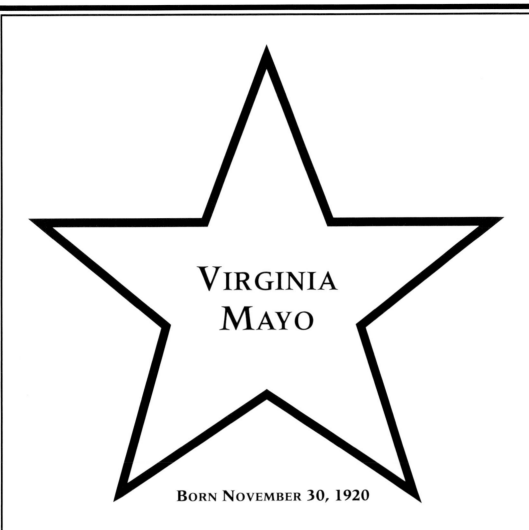

VIRGINIA MAYO

BORN NOVEMBER 30, 1920

Noted for her striking beauty, Virginia Mayo was one of the most successful actresses of the 1940s and 1950s. Born Virginia Jones in St. Louis, she began training at her aunt's drama school at age six. She graduated from Soldan High School and danced for the Muny Opera before Samuel Goldwyn signed her to a Hollywood contract. Mayo made almost 50 movies, including *White Heat, She's Working Her Way Through College,* and *The Best Years of Our Lives,* and appeared in 20 stage productions and many TV shows. Called "tangible proof of God's existence" by the Sultan of Morocco, Virginia Mayo received one of the original stars on Hollywood Boulevard.

MARIANNE MOORE

BORN NOVEMBER 15, 1887

Born in Kirkwood, poet Marianne Moore was profoundly influenced by her early upbringing in the St. Louis area before her family moved to Pennsylvania. One of the most influential early modernists and an inspiration to generations of women poets, Moore is known for her keen sense of detail and her precise use of language. She published many volumes of acclaimed poetry in 50 years, including *Collected Works* (1951), which won a Pulitzer Prize and a National Book Award. Also an essayist and translator, Moore was modest and skeptical of her own writing, but others saw her genius. T. S. Eliot said the work of Marianne Moore is "part of the small body of durable poetry."

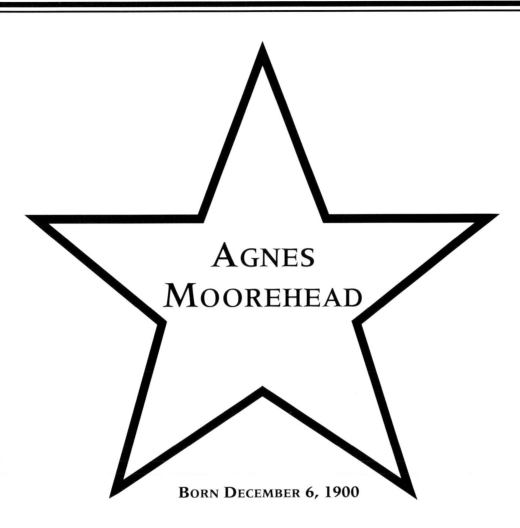

AGNES
MOOREHEAD

BORN DECEMBER 6, 1900

Agnes Moorehead moved to St. Louis as a child, where she acted in stage productions, danced with the Municipal Opera, and debuted as a radio singer on KMOX in 1923. After moving to New York and appearing on Broadway, she became a charter member of Orson Welles' famous Mercury Theater, starring in hundreds of radio dramas. Following her 1941 movie debut in *Citizen Kane*, she displayed her range as a character actress in over 60 films and also played Endora on TV's "Bewitched" from 1964-1972. One of the best acting voices in radio history, Agnes Moorehead also received four nominations for Academy Awards.

STAN MUSIAL

BORN NOVEMBER 21, 1920

Stan Musial was one of the greatest players in the history of baseball. A gentleman both on the field and off, "Stan the Man" played his entire 22 year professional career with the St. Louis Cardinals. He had a lifetime .331 batting average, with 3630 base hits and 475 home runs, and held numerous records when he retired. Musial won seven league batting titles and three Most Valuable Player awards, and helped the Cardinals win three world championships. He was inducted into the Baseball Hall of Fame in 1969.

HOWARD NEMEROV

BORN MARCH 1, 1920

Howard Nemerov graduated from Harvard in 1941, served in World War II, and began teaching in 1946. His first volume of poetry, *The Image and the Law*, was published the next year. In 1969, he became professor of English at Washington University. In addition to 13 volumes of poetry, his works include novels, stories and a notable body of criticism. He was inducted into the American Academy and Institute of Arts and Letters in 1977. T*he Collected Poems of Howard Nemerov* won The National Book Award and the Pulitzer Prize a year later. He was named Poet Laureate of the United States in 1988.

GYO
OBATA

BORN FEBRUARY 28, 1923

Gyo Obata, a Washington University graduate, co-founded the St. Louis architecture firm Hellmuth, Obata & Kassabaum in 1955. It attained global prominence, largely due to Obata's designs. His influence on the St. Louis skyline is profound. The Priory Chapel, Boatmen's Tower, Cervantes Convention Center & Stadium, Forsythe Plaza, Metropolitan Square, One Bell Center, the Children's Zoo and Living World, and the Union Station renovation are but a few of Obata's St. Louis projects. The National Air and Space Museum, the airport and university in Riyadh, Saudi Arabia, and the Taipei World Trade Center exemplify the worldwide work of Gyo Obata.

MARLIN PERKINS

BORN MARCH 28, 1902

Marlin Perkins came to the St. Louis Zoo in 1926 to work with the reptile collection. He became curator of the Buffalo Zoo in 1938. As director of Chicago's Lincoln Park Zoo in 1949, he created the Peabody Award-winning television show "Zoo Parade." In 1962 Perkins returned to the St. Louis Zoo as director. He debuted "Wild Kingdom" in 1963, hosting it until 1985. Winner of four Emmy Awards, it taught a generation about animals in their habitats and is in the Television Hall of Fame. The American Association of Zoological Parks & Aquariums' top honor for achievement has been named the "Marlin Perkins Award."

VINCENT PRICE

BORN MAY 27, 1911

Called "The King of Horror," Vincent Price is best known for his villainous roles in more than 100 films, as well as many stage and television productions, but his accomplishments cover a much broader range. He is a connoisseur of fine art and the author of a number of books on the subject. A collector as well, he bought a Rembrandt drawing at age twelve, while still living in the family house on Forsyth Blvd. Price, who is also the author of several gourmet cookbooks, graduated from Community School and St. Louis Country Day School.

JOSEPH PULITZER

BORN APRIL 10, 1847

A native of Hungary, Joseph Pulitzer emigrated to the U.S. in 1864 and served in the Union Army during the Civil War. He moved to St. Louis in 1868 to work as a reporter for a German-language newspaper. He bought the bankrupt *St. Louis Dispatch* in 1878 and soon merged it with the *Evening Post* to form the *St. Louis Post-Dispatch*. Pulitzer, an exponent of high journalistic standards, endowed the Columbia School of Journalism. His greatest legacy is his annual award for excellence in journalism—the Pulitzer Prize.

PETER RAVEN

BORN JUNE 13, 1936

Born in China, Peter Raven was a professor at Stanford University before moving to St. Louis in 1971 to head the Missouri Botanical Garden. Under his direction, it became the leading tropical plant research facility in the world, its staff racing to catalog species doomed to extinction. Raven stressed that the destruction of each rainforest is "one more step toward creating a world in which we cannot live." A preeminent scientist and professor at Washington University, Peter Raven became a world-renowned champion of the environment, lecturing around the globe and writing dozens of books and articles to stop man's decimation of life-giving plants.

BRANCH RICKEY

BORN DECEMBER 20, 1881

Often called the greatest front-office strategist in baseball history, Branch Rickey came to the Cardinals in 1917 and turned a losing team into a powerhouse. Believing that "luck is the residue of design," he developed the modern farm system that brought the Cardinals nine pennants and six World Series through the 1940s. After moving to the Brooklyn Dodgers, Rickey signed Jackie Robinson and brought him to the majors in 1947; more black players soon followed. Branch Rickey simultaneously broke baseball's color line and built the great Dodger teams of the 1940s and 1950s, ensuring his induction into the Baseball Hall of Fame.

CHARLES RUSSELL

BORN MARCH 19, 1864

Charles Marion Russell's more than 3,000 paintings, drawings and sculptures captured the essence of the American West. Born in St. Louis, he grew up at Oak Hill, his family's country estate near present-day Tower Grove Park. Russell, who moved to Montana at age 15 to be a cowboy, was a professional artist by 1893. Within a decade he was nationally recognized for the accuracy with which he rendered his subjects. Russell was also an able storyteller, whom Will Rogers called the best he ever heard. One of the premier artists of the American West, Charles M. Russell lovingly preserved the rugged splendor of the frontier.

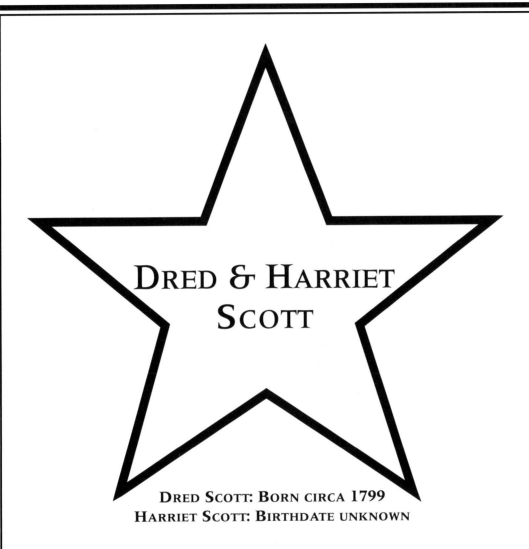

DRED & HARRIET SCOTT

DRED SCOTT: BORN CIRCA 1799
HARRIET SCOTT: BIRTHDATE UNKNOWN

Remembered for the infamous 1857 decision that denied them their freedom, Dred and Harriet Scott spent much of their adult lives enslaved in St. Louis. In the 1830s, Dred Scott's slave owner took him to the free state of Illinois and then to federal territory, where slavery was prohibited. While there, he married Harriet. They were returned to St. Louis in 1838, and in 1846 began a courageous 11-year legal battle for emancipation based on their time spent in free territory. The U.S. Supreme Court's decision withheld the fundamental rights of citizenship from Dred and Harriet Scott—and all black Americans—propelling the nation toward civil war.

HENRY SHAW

BORN JULY 24, 1800

Henry Shaw, only 18 when he came to St. Louis, was one of the city's largest landowners by age 40. Working with leading botanists, he planned, funded and built the Missouri Botanical Garden, which opened in 1859. Shaw donated the land for Tower Grove Park and helped with its construction. He wrote botanical tracts, endowed Washington University's School of Botany, helped found the Missouri Historical Society, and gave the city a school and land for a hospital. Of Shaw's gifts, the Botanical Garden is best-known. Said as early as 1868 to have "no equal in the United States, and, indeed, few anywhere in the world," it epitomizes the legacy of Henry Shaw.

LEONARD SLATKIN

BORN SEPTEMBER 1, 1944

Leonard Slatkin studied violin, viola and piano as a child, and made his Carnegie Hall conducting debut at age 22. The leading American conductor of his generation, he was named music director of the Saint Louis Symphony Orchestra in 1979. He has earned critical praise for his work here and with ensembles around the globe. Slatkin and the symphony have received wide acclaim, including numerous Grammy nominations and awards. Lauded for his commitment to American music, adventurous programming, and superb performances and recordings, Leonard Slatkin has emerged as one of the world's great conductors.

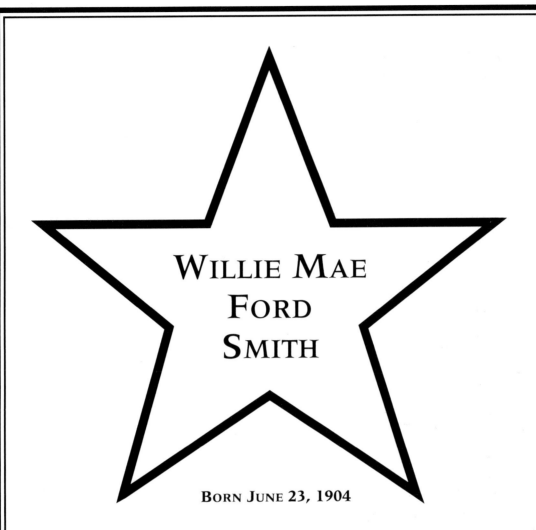

WILLIE MAE FORD SMITH

BORN JUNE 23, 1904

The music we now call gospel was thought too worldly in 1917 when Willie Mae Ford moved to St. Louis, but she was to change that. Rather than deny the power of the blues, she enfolded it in her religious convictions to form a joyous new message of praise. Having helped found the National Convention of Gospel Choirs and Choruses, she organized its Soloists' Bureau in 1939. Profoundly influencing almost every gospel singer to follow, she was featured in the 1983 film Say Amen, Somebody. Willie Mae Ford Smith received the Heritage Award from the National Endowment for the Arts In 1988.

SARA
TEASDALE

BORN AUGUST 8, 1884

Sara Teasdale was born in St. Louis and lived both on Lindell Blvd. and on Kingsbury Place. While attending Mary Institute and Hosmer Hall, she began writing poems. First published in 1907, Teasdale wrote several collections of poetry in the following decade and became known for the intensity of her lyrics. In 1918 *Love Songs* won what was essentially the first Pulitzer Prize for Poetry. Expressing disenchantment with marriage, Teasdale's later poetry resonated with suffering and strength. According to one biographer, Sara Teasdale spoke for "women emerging from the humility of subservience into the pride of achievement."

CLARK TERRY

BORN DECEMBER 14, 1920

Born in St. Louis, Clark Terry made his first trumpet out of garden hose, attended Vashon High School, and played in local clubs before joining a Navy band during World War II. His years with Count Basie and Duke Ellington in the late 1940s and 1950s established him as a world-class jazz artist. Blending the St. Louis tone of his youth with contemporary styles, Terry's sound influenced a generation, including Miles Davis. Also a pioneer of the fluegelhorn in jazz, Terry was a standout in the NBC-TV Orchestra for 12 years before he left to form his own bands and continue recording. Clark Terry was inducted into the National Endowment for the Arts Jazz Hall of Fame in 1991.

HENRY TOWNSEND

BORN OCTOBER 27, 1909

A great blues guitarist and pianist, Henry Townsend grew up near Cairo, Illinois. After moving to St. Louis, he made his first record in 1929. During the 1930s, he played with many of the early blues giants, including Walter Davis, Roosevelt Sykes and Robert Johnson. The author of hundreds of songs and sideman on countless recordings, Townsend became the patriarch of St. Louis blues, was featured in a BBC documentary, and recorded in each of eight decades. Recognized as a "master artist," he received the National Heritage Award in 1985. *Blues Unlimited* magazine called Henry Townsend "a commanding genius of a musician."

HELEN TRAUBEL

BORN JUNE 16, 1899

Born above her father's drugstore at Jefferson and Chouteau Avenues in south St. Louis, heroic-voiced Helen Traubel debuted with the St. Louis Symphony in 1924. To continue her training in St. Louis, she initially declined an offer from New York's Metropolitan Opera, but moved to New York in the late 1930s. Traubel was the Met's premier Wagnerian soprano until she left in 1953 to appear in nightclubs, on television and in movies. With her joyous confidence and booming laughter, Helen Traubel broke down barriers in a stratified society and proved that an American could succeed in the European-dominated opera world.

ERNEST TROVA

BORN FEBRUARY 19, 1927

Ernest Tino Trova, a self-trained St. Louis native, became one of the significant artists of the late twentieth century. Best known for his signature image, the *Falling Man*, Trova considered his entire output a single "work in progress." A collector of classic American comic character toys, Trova admired their surrealism and used them in some of his pieces. He began as a painter, progressing through three-dimensional constructions to his mature medium, sculpture. Trova's gift of forty of his works led to the opening of the Laumeier Sculpture Park. With his *Falling Man*, Ernest Trova created one of the defining artistic images of his time.

TINA TURNER

BORN NOVEMBER 26, 1939

Her powerful voice and the raw intensity of her stage shows brought Tina Turner rhythm & blues fame in the 1960s. Born Anna Mae Bullock in Nutbush, Tennessee, she moved to St. Louis at age 16. She was a student at Sumner High School when she joined Ike Turner and the Kings of Rhythm. With the 1960 hit "A Fool In Love," they became the Ike & Tina Turner Revue. In 1977 Tina left to pursue a solo career that took her to the top of the Pop, Rock and R & B charts. She won three 1984 Grammy Awards, including Record of the Year for "What's Love Got To Do With It." In 1991 Tina Turner was inducted into the Rock & Roll Hall of Fame.

MONA VAN DUYN

BORN MAY 9, 1921

In 1947 Mona Van Duyn co-founded *Perspective: A Quarterly of Literature* with her husband, Jarvis Thurston. Moving to St. Louis in 1950, they published it for another 30 years. Van Duyn's first book of poetry, *Valentines to the Wide World*, was published in 1959. One of the nation's preeminent poets, she won the Bollingen Prize, the National Book Award, the Academy of American Poets fellowship and the Ruth Lilly Award. Van Duyn, whose poetry finds large truths in small subjects, won the 1991 Pulitzer Prize for poetry for her seventh book, *Near Changes*. In 1992 Mona Van Duyn was named Poet Laureate of the United States.

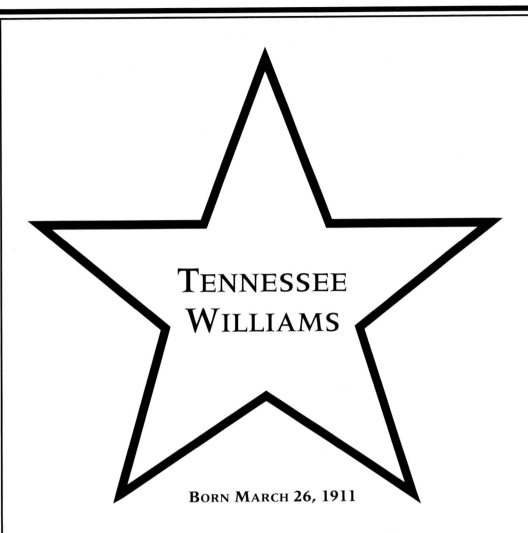

TENNESSEE WILLIAMS

BORN MARCH 26, 1911

One of the greatest twentieth century playwrights, Tennessee Williams attended Soldan and University City high schools, and Washington University, before graduating from the University of Iowa. His plays explore what he called "the unlighted sides" of human nature with great insight. He won Pulitzer Prizes for *Streetcar Named Desire* and *Cat On A Hot Tin Roof.* Those works, along with *Glass Menagerie* and *Night of the Iguana*, also won New York Drama Critics Circle Awards. Williams wrote nearly thirty full-length plays, two novels, and a number of short stories and plays.

SHELLEY WINTERS

BORN AUGUST 18, 1920

Born Shirley Schrift in an apartment on Newstead Ave. in St. Louis, she was in the Veiled Prophet pageant at age four. She left high school to become a model, studying acting at night. A gifted performer who fought Hollywood's stereotypes, Shelley Winters earned an Oscar nomination for the 1945 film *Double Life*, her first major role. Devoted to Method acting, she appeared in 50 plays as well as more than 100 films and television shows. A frequent award nominee, she received a 1964 Emmy for *Two Is the Number*. Shelley Winters won two Academy Awards, for *The Diary of Anne Frank* in 1959 and *A Patch of Blue* in 1965.

ACKNOWLEDGEMENTS

PROJECT DIRECTOR: Joe Edwards

EDITING: Tom Peckham, Brad Hines

RESEARCH/TEXT: Brad Hines, Karin Steinmeyer, Carol Conway-Long,
Mary Ann Fitzgerald, Phil Carmody, Tom Peckham, Joe Edwards.

PHOTO CREDITS:
Cover Photo: Photographic Resources / Frank Oberle.

Missouri Historical Society, St. Louis: Josephine Baker, Susan Blow, Kate Chopin, Auguste Chouteau, William Clark, Carl & Gerty Cori, T.S. Eliot, Eugene Field, Ulysses S. Grant (photograph by G. Cramer), Pierre Laclede, Theodore Link, Charles M. Russell (photograph by Pollard), Willie Mae Ford Smith, Sara Teasdale, Helen Traubel.

Washington University/Herb Weitman: Howard Nemerov, Mona Van Duyn,
Arthur Holly Compton.

Elijah Parish Lovejoy Society: Elijah Lovejoy.

Scott Joplin State Historic Site: Scott Joplin.

St. Louis Post-Dispatch: Portrait of Joseph Pulitzer by John Singer Sargent,
photographed by D. Gulick.

Portrait Collection, Missouri Botanical Garden, Library:
painting of Henry Shaw by Fairchild & Rox.

From The Collections of The St. Louis Mercantile Library Association: Henry Armstrong, Yogi Berra, Lou Brock, Harry Caray, Dizzy Dean, Katherine Dunham, James B. Eads, Charles Eames, Redd Foxx, David Garroway, Bob Gibson, Betty Grable, Al Hirschfeld, William Inge, Charles Lindbergh, Bill Mauldin, Marianne Moore, Agnes Moorehead, Stan Musial, Vincent Price, Branch Rickey, Dred & Harriet Scott, Clark Terry, Tina Turner, Tennessee Williams.

Wart Enterprizes/David Horwitz©: Albert King.

Richard Martin: Josephine Baker.

Jackie Jackson: Willie Mae Ford Smith.

H.O.K.: Gyo Obata.

Henry Townsend photograph by Bill Greensmith Photography.

Stanley Elkin photograph by Joan Elkin.

Masters & Johnson photograph by Buzz Taylor.

Jack Buck photograph by Larry Sherron.

PHOTOGRAPHS OF INDUCTION CEREMONIES: Jennifer Silverberg, Drea Stein.

CEREMONY MUSIC: Original St. Louis River Critters Jazz Band.

ANNUAL WALK OF FAME WINDOW DISPLAY: Linda Edwards.

COMMUNITY SUPPORT

☆ ☆ ☆ ☆

WE INVITE YOU TO BECOME A SUPPORTING MEMBER of this non-profit 501(c)(3) project, that brings pride, knowledge and inspiration to St. Louisans year after year.

New supporters who contribute $35 or more will receive a certificate of commendation suitable for framing, with a Walk of Fame inductee as honorary signatory.

Patrons who donate $250 or more will have their names added to the following list of supporters in future editions of this book, along with other benefits.

CONTRIBUTORS

WITH SPECIAL SUPPORT FROM
THE REGIONAL ARTS COMMISSION
AND
THE UNIVERSITY CITY LOOP S.B.D.

PRIVATE CONTRIBUTORS

Anonymous
Chuck Berry
Ed Brimer
Bill Bueler
Bill & Betty Carroll
Jeff Clinton
Jerry Clinton
Jim Damos
Joe & Nancy deBettencourt
Joe & Linda Edwards
Ed Finkelstein
Mark & Mary Gorman
Salim Hanna
Ray Hartmann
Rose Jonas
Dennis Lutsky
John D. Mandelker
Eric & Claudia Mink
Carol Perkins
Thomas J. Purcell, Jr.
Leon & Ann Robison
Pete & Donna Rothschild
Eleanor Ruder
Rick Schaumberger
Sondra & Milton Schlesinger
Paul & Suzanne Schoomer
Sid Stone
Steve Stone
Greg Sullivan
Dan & Robin Wald
Lana Wald
Sam Wald
David Weiss
Allan Welge
Jerry & Sandy Wool

COMMERCIAL CONTRIBUTORS

AdVentures Screenprinting
Backstage Galleries
Blueberry Hill
Cicero's
Coolaire Company
Commerce Bancshares Foundation
Commerce Bank of University City
Componere Gallery
Craft Alliance Gallery
Engraphix
Fitz's Bottling Co.
G.A. Sullivan
Grey Eagle Distributors
H.S.B. Tobacconist
Loop Subway
Photographic Resources
Plowsharing Crafts
Pulitzer Publishing Co. Foundation
Carl Safe Design Consultants
Saleem's Restaurant
Signature Beer Co.
Streetside Records
Tivoli Theatre
Wonder Novelty

> **SPECIAL THANKS** to former Mayor Janet Majerus, members of the Council and the citizens of University City for providing the sidewalks of the U. City Loop as the location for the St. Louis Walk of Fame.